I'm Reading About

ARKANSAS

The Natural State!

GALLOPADE

by Carole Marsh

Printed and Manufactured in Peachtree City, GA., USA
www.gallopade.com

Book design: John Hanson

Editorial manager: Janice Baker

Arkansas is a great state.
It is one of a kind.

What makes Arkansas special?
Let's read about it
and see!

NATIVE AMERICANS

Who lived in Arkansas first?

Native Americans did!

They moved around to find food.
They hunted in Arkansas' woods.
They fished in Arkansas' rivers.
They gathered fruits and seeds and nuts.

EXPLORERS

The first explorers came to Arkansas in 1541.
They came from the country of Spain.

Hernando de Soto was their leader.
He and his men were looking for cities of gold!

SETTLEMENT

A man named Henri de Tonti came
from France to America.
He started the first settlement in Arkansas.
He named it Arkansas Post.

Arkansas Post was built along
the Arkansas River.

Arkansas Post

STATEHOOD

Arkansas was the 25th state
to join the United States of America!

Isn't it great,
to be a state!
I bet Arkansas
could hardly wait!

Arkansas became a state in 1836.

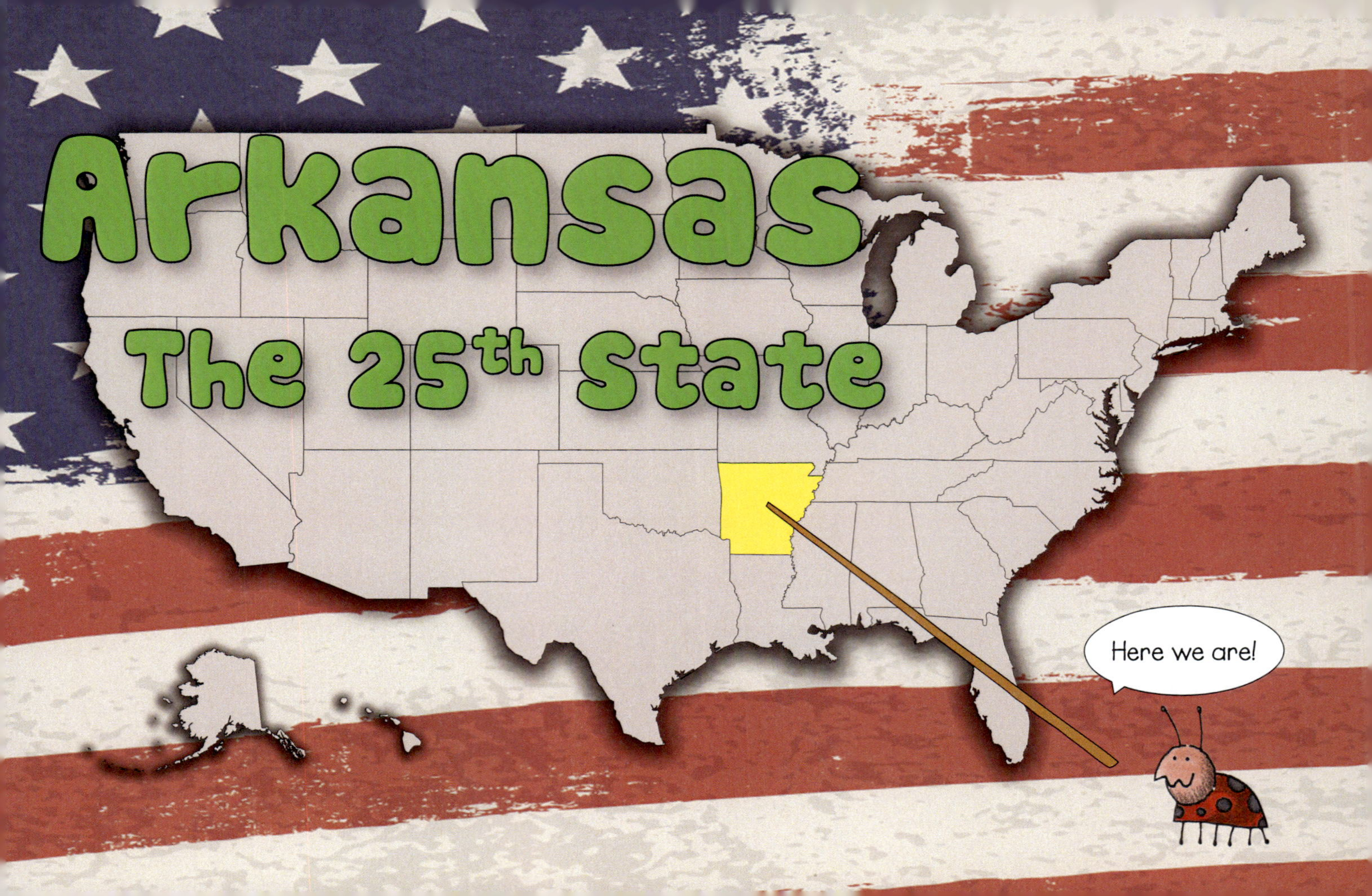
Arkansas
The 25th State
Here we are!

FLAG

I am the state flag.
I was adopted in 1924.

What colors am I?
Red. White. Blue.

Look at me.
What else do you see?

I fly high over the state of Arkansas!

ARKANSAS

CAPITAL

Say hello to Little Rock,
the capital city of Arkansas!

There is an important building in Little Rock.
It is the State Capitol.
Arkansas' laws are made there!

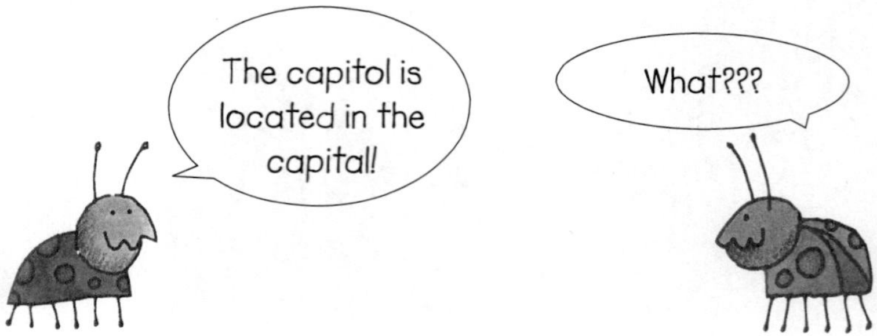

Capitol

SEAL

I am a seal,
but I am not the State Seal.
If I were, I would be very important.
I would be stamped on many official papers.
(Ouch, that might hurt!)

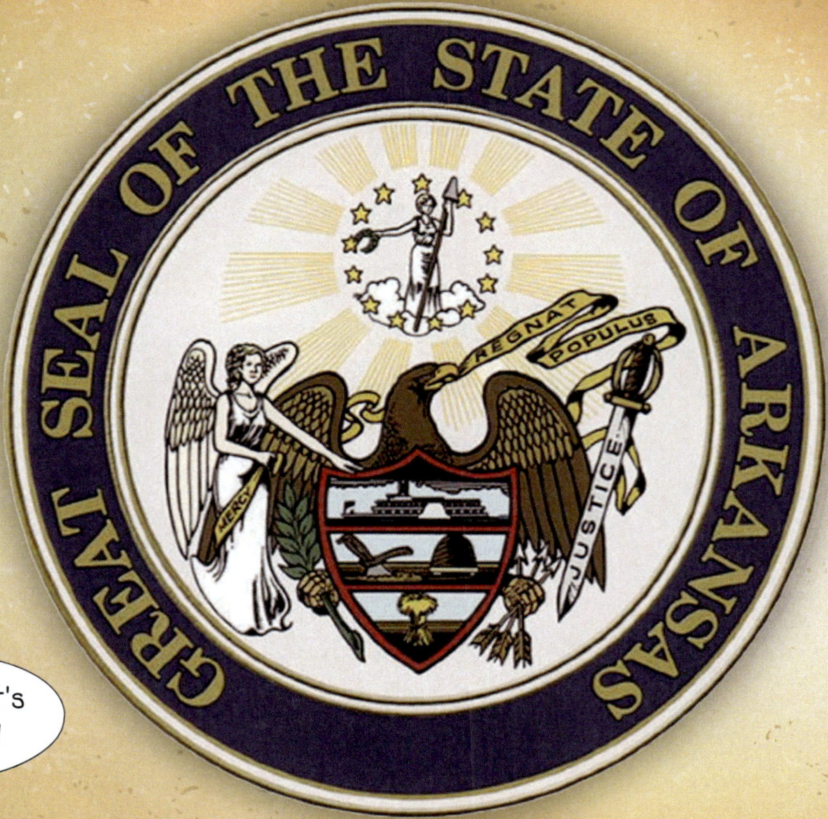
GREAT SEAL OF THE STATE OF ARKANSAS
REGNAT POPULUS
MERCY
JUSTICE

Now, that's official!

NICKNAME

State nicknames are fun!
State nicknames are great!
They share fun facts
about each state!

Arkansas' nickname is "The Natural State."

Arkansas has beautiful natural scenery—lakes, rivers, mountains, and more!

The Natural State

BORDERS

Look at Arkansas.
Arkansas is in a region called "the South."

Arkansas borders six other states.
Find them on the map!

Borders

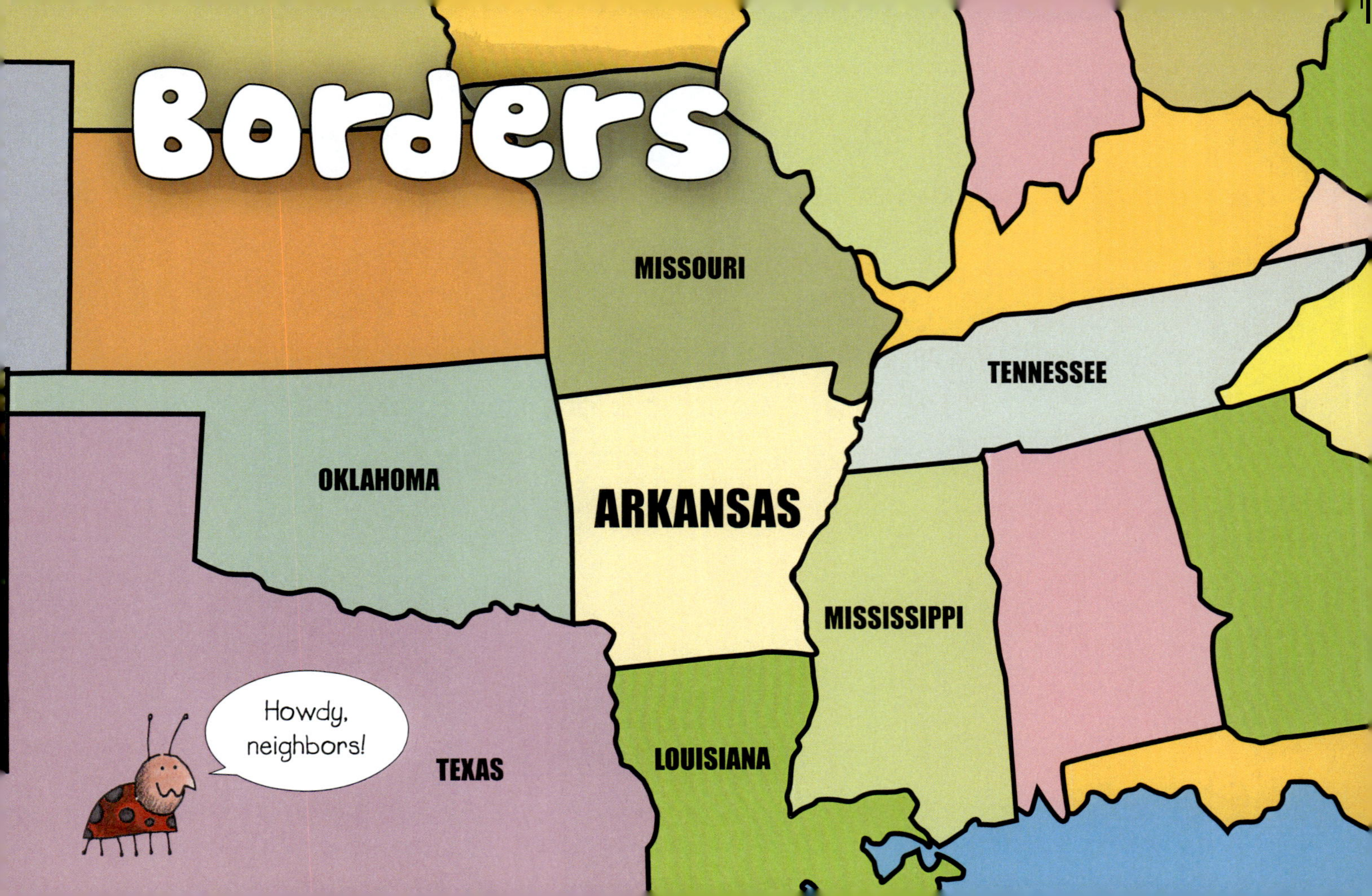
MISSOURI
TENNESSEE
OKLAHOMA
ARKANSAS
MISSISSIPPI
Howdy, neighbors!
TEXAS
LOUISIANA

PRESIDENT

Bill Clinton was the 42nd President
of the United States of America.
He was born in Arkansas!

Bill Clinton grew up in a town called Hot Springs.
He was a good student and loved music.
He played the saxophone in his school band!

Bill Clinton

PEOPLE

Many famous people

Hattie Caraway

First woman elected to the U.S. Senate

General Douglas MacArthur

Supreme Commander of the Allied Forces during World War II

Paul "Bear" Bryant

College football coach who won six national championships

call our state home!

Sam Walton
Founder of Walmart

Maya Angelou
Poet, actress, and singer

Johnny Cash
Musician who mixed country, rock, blues, and gospel styles

Mockingbird

I am the state bird, and I fly
over Arkansas, proud and high.

As I fly, up in the sky,
I flap my wings to tell you "Hi!"

The Arkansas state bird is the Mockingbird.

BIRD

Apple
Blossom

FLOWER

I am the Apple Blossom.
I am the state flower.

I grow where it's warm and sunny.
I bloom in early spring.
I help make Arkansas beautiful!

Look at me! Smell me!
I bloom on the apple tree.

Pine

TREE

I am a Pine—I'm the state tree.
All over Arkansas is where to find me.

My roots run deep, they keep me strong.
My leaves stay green, all year long.

I stand up straight, big and tall.
Don't climb too high—it would hurt to fall!

Honeybee

INSECT

I am the Honeybee.
I am the state insect.

I might sting you if you bother me.
But really, I am your friend.

I carry pollen from flower to flower.
I make honey.
I help Arkansas crops grow.

BZZZZZZZZZZZ!

Lakes

LAKES

Let's go to the lake!

We can wade in the water.
We can ride on a boat.

We can jump off the dock
onto an inner tube float!

Arkansas lakes are home to many animals:

Fish **Snakes** **Birds** **Turtles** **Salamanders** **and More!**

Ozark Mountains

MOUNTAINS

Arkansas' Ozark Mountains are the place to be.
Hiking, fishing, camping—
fun for you and me.

If you were to climb
to the top of a tree,
you'd have a very nice view to see!

Rivers

RIVERS

Arkansas has many rivers.
People like to use the rivers for boating and fishing!

This habitat is home to many animals:

Birds Deer Snakes Frogs Fish and More!

The first explorers to Arkansas traveled down rivers.

Hot Springs National Park

LANDMARK

Hot Springs National Park is located in central Arkansas. The hot water is heated underground. Then, it flows down from Hot Springs Mountain. Many people have used the hot springs to soothe ailments!

Native Americans called the hot springs area the "Valley of the Vapors."

Arkansas Crops

AGRICULTURE

Arkansas has many farms.
Why?
Because Arkansas has good soil and a warm climate!

Some of the top crops grown in Arkansas are:

Rice **Soybeans** **Cotton** **Wheat**

Hey!
Don't forget about me!
I am a young chicken.
They call me a "broiler."
Arkansas raises lots of broilers!

Sports in Arkansas

SPORTS

Baseball! Basketball! Football!
Arkansas has it all.

Whether you like to watch or play,
You are sure to have a ball!

Razorbacks **Trojans**

Golden Lions

Red Wolves

& More!

Arkansas: Home of Walmart

CLAIM TO FAME

Arkansas is home to Walmart!
Walmart is the largest retail company in the world.
People can buy groceries and other
household goods at Walmart.
It's a good place for "one-stop" shopping!

Bananas are one of Walmart's best-selling items!

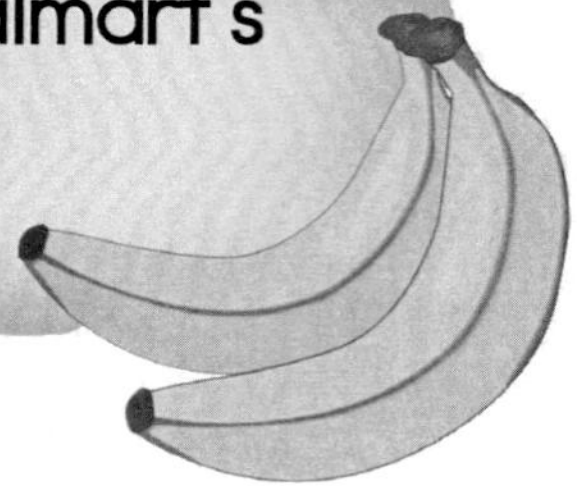

GLOSSARY

ailment: an illness, typically a minor one

climate: weather conditions in an area over a long period of time

elect: to choose someone by voting

habitat: a place where plants or animals naturally live

laws: rules made by the government

pollen: a yellow powder that helps plants make new plants

region: an area that has similar characteristics

retail: the sale of goods and services from businesses to consumers

scenery: a view of the natural features of land that is pleasing to look at

settlement: the first community in an area